The Egyptians

Written by Sally Hewitt

W

FRANKLIN WATTS

LONDON·SYDNEY

First published in 2006 by Franklin Watts
338 Euston Road, London NW1 3BH

Franklin Watts Australia
Level 17/207 Kent Street, Sydney NSW 2000

Editor: Rachel Tonkin
Designers: Rachel Hamdi and Holly Fulbrook
Picture researcher: Diana Morris
Craft models made by: Anna-Marie D'Cruz
Map artwork: Ian Thompson

Picture credits
Bettmann/Corbis: 15t; Dagli Orti/Art Archive: front cover t; Dagli
Orti/Art Archive/Corbis: 12tr, 16t, 16b; Werner Forman Archive:
6, 7t, 12bl, 17t, 18, 21t; Werner Forman/Corbis: 7b; Hutchison/Eye
Ubiquitous: 8; Ladislav Janicek/zefa/Corbis: 22c; Charles & Josette
Lenars/Corbis: 11t, 14r, 26bl; Paul C. Pet/zefa/Corbis: 20l; Jose
Fuste Raga/Corbis: 22b; Topfoto: 23t, 24, 26cr; Sandro
Vianni/Corbis: 27t; Roger Wood/Corbis: 10, 20r, 25t.

All other images: Steve Shott

With thanks to our models Maria Cheung and Ryan Lovett

A CIP catalogue record for this book
is available from the British Library

ISBN: 978 0 7496 6497 8

Dewey Classification: 932

Printed in China

Franklin Watts is a division of Hachette Children's Books.

Contents

The Egyptians

The Ancient Egyptians lived near the banks of the River Nile in Egypt. There was plenty of water and the soil was good for farming. Their **civilisation** started in 3,100 BCE and ended in 30 BCE when Egypt became part of the Roman Empire.

Egyptian civilisation

The Egyptians were ruled by a king called a **pharaoh**. They were clever **engineers** who built cities with magnificent palaces, temples and **tombs**.

The remains of pots, weapons, tools and jewellery found show that they were also skilled craftsmen.

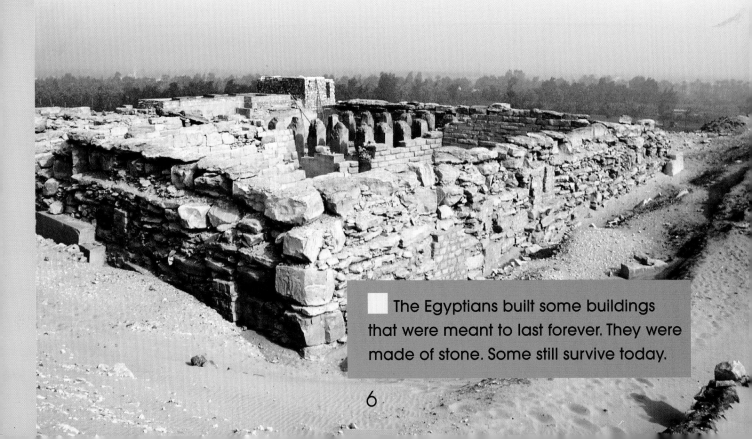

The Egyptians built some buildings that were meant to last forever. They were made of stone. Some still survive today.

Trade

Egypt was a wealthy country. Egyptian traders sold their **goods** to Africa, the Mediterranean and far-away India. They brought back exotic animals, ivory, timber, silk and perfume.

 This Egyptian wall painting shows images of people trading goods and animals.

This is a model of the type of boat Egyptians sailed in to trade goods.

The River Nile

The River Nile is the longest river in the world. It runs through the North African desert and out into the Mediterranean Sea.

Floods

Snow melting in the mountains in the south floods the Nile every year in June. The floodwater leaves behind **silt** which makes the soil good for farming.

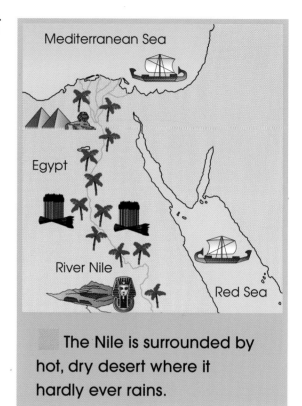

The Nile is surrounded by hot, dry desert where it hardly ever rains.

The Ancient Egyptians used shadufs to lift water from the canals. Shadufs are still used today.

Farming

The Ancient Egyptians settled along the banks of the River Nile and farmers planted crops in the rich soil. Their year was divided into three seasons called flood, crop sowing and harvesting. As there was little rain, farmers cut **irrigation canals** to carry water from the river to the fields and villages.

Make a shaduf

▶ **1** Tie together three sticks of square dowel, about 20 cm long, 3 cm from one end. Spread them into a triangular frame. Press the ends into a Plasticine base.

▶ **4** Shape a bucket from foil. Hang it from the other end of the lever with a piece of long string.

▶ **2** Loosely tie a 30 cm stick of square dowel, about 4 cm from one end, to the top of the frame.

▶ **3** Add a lump of Plasticine to make a counterweight to the short end.

Try it out. Pull the string down to fill the bucket with water. Push down on the weight to lift the bucket of water.

Egyptian life

Keeping cool and growing enough food to eat was an important part of Egyptian daily life.

Nobles to slaves

Wealthy **nobles** served in the Pharaoh's court. Educated **scribes** kept important records and priests ran the temples. There were many traders and skilled craftsmen but most people were peasants who belonged to the landowners. There were a few **slaves**.

Houses

Keeping cool was an

Houses were made from mud bricks strengthened with straw and baked hard in the sun. You can still find houses in Egypt made like this.

important part of daily life for the Egyptians. Their houses were built to keep out the heat. The walls were painted white to reflect the sun. Windows were small and high and vents in the roofs and walls trapped the cool North winds.

After feasting, rich Egyptians enjoyed music. They used fans to cool themselves as they listened.

Food

Rich soil alongside the Nile meant the Egyptians could grow lots of food for festivals and feasts. Bread and cakes were made from wheat and barley. Figs, dates and grapes were either eaten fresh, or dried and stored, or made into wine. They caught fish from the river.

Make a fan

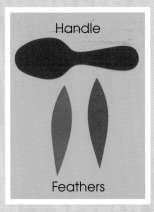

Handle

Feathers

▶ 1 Cut out about 30 feather shapes (left) from white card, about 16 cm long.

▶ 4 Stick the white feathers onto the back of the handle, adding the coloured feathers to make a pattern. Use your fan to keep cool.

▶ 2 Cut out feathers in gold, purple and green card, three in each colour.

▶ 3 Copy and cut out the handle (above) from strong brown card. Make it 20 cm long.

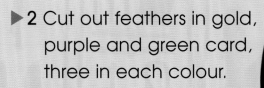

Clothes

Egyptian clothes were made from **linen**. They were light and loose for keeping cool in the heat. Men's **kilts** and women's dresses were often pressed into pleats. Farmers wore **loin cloths** to work in the fields while children ran around naked in the heat.

Clothes were usually white, the natural colour of the linen cloth, like the Egyptians are wearing in this wall painting.

Linen

Linen was made from the fibres of the flax plant. First the flax heads were removed with a type of comb. Then the stems were soaked, beaten and combed until they were ready for spinning into thread.

Nets

Nets helped to protect linen clothes from wearing out too quickly. Soldiers wore leather nets over their kilts and women servants wore beaded nets over their dresses.

This is one of the oldest existing items of clothing. It is an Egyptian linen shirt.

Make Egyptian sandals

The Egyptians wore sandals which were made from papyrus – a kind of reed that grows on the banks of the Nile.

▶ **1** Draw round your feet on a piece of thick cardboard. Mark two spots between your big toe and second toe. Mark a spot on either side of the heel.

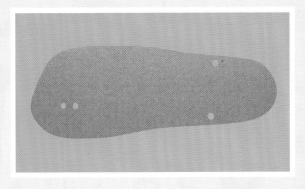

▶ **2** Ask an adult to help you cut them out and punch holes on the marked spots.

▶ **3** Tie two 10 cm long pieces of brown ribbon in the holes by the heel, one in each.

▶ **4** Thread a 40 cm long piece of brown ribbon down and back up through the holes by the toes.

▶ **5** Pull the ribbon so it is equal lengths and knot. To make the bit to go between your toes, tie the ribbon together again 6 cm along.

▶ **6** Tie the ends of the ribbons in bows around your foot. Finish the sandal for your other foot and try them on.

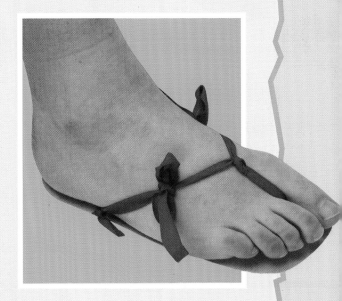

Hair and make-up

Most Egyptians wore some jewellery. Ordinary people wore copper rings and **amulets** to keep away evil spirits. Jewellery for wealthy Egyptians was made of gold from Egypt's own gold mines. Collars, rings, ear studs, bracelets and **anklets** were set with colourful semi-precious stones.

Make-up

The Egyptians used mirrors, combs, tweezers and make-up to help them to look their best. Coloured minerals were ground into powder and mixed with wax to make black eye paint and red rouge for lips and cheeks.

Wigs and wax

Egyptians wore long, black, plaited wigs. A cone of scented wax worn on top of the head melted in the heat and trickled down the wearer's wig, making them smell nice.

Both men and women outlined their eyes with black make-up.

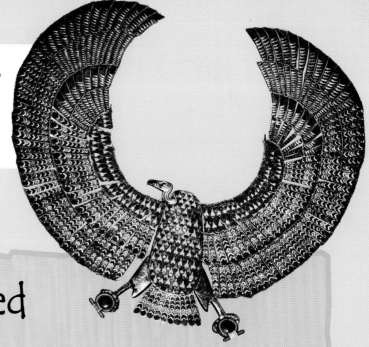

■ Craftsmen moulded, beat and carved metal into jewellery like this collar.

Make a decorated collar

Decorated collars added richness and colour to the plain linen clothes.

▶ 1 Copy the shape of the collar. Make it as wide as your shoulders. Punch holes in the top as shown.

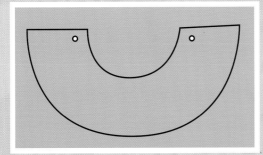

▶ 2 Cut coloured straws into 2-cm lengths. Decorate the collar with alternate stripes of paint, rows of coloured straws and sequins.

▶ 3 Thread with ribbon and wear your Egyptian collar.

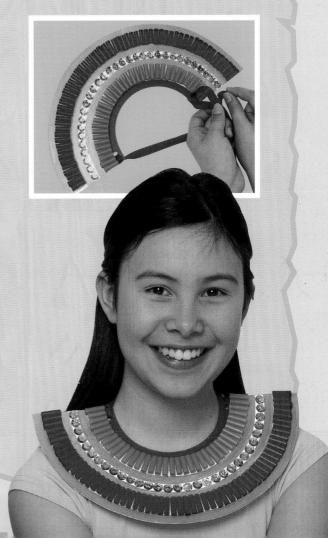

Writing

The Ancient Egyptians wrote in **hieroglyphs**. Some of the words looked like pictures. For hundreds of years, historians could not understand the hieroglyphs.

In 1799, the Rosetta stone was found. The same words were written in three different languages: Greek, Demotic and hieroglyphs. This meant that scholars could now translate hieroglyphs for the first time.

The Rosetta stone unlocked the ancient secrets of the hieroglyphs.

Scribes wrote hieroglyphs on papyrus or carved them in stone.

Scribes

Very few people could read and write hieroglyphs. There were about 700 signs to learn. Scribes started their training as young boys and took many years to learn to read and write hieroglyphs.

Papyrus

Papyrus was a kind of paper made of pith from the stem of the papyrus reed. Strips of pith were laid criss-cross on a frame and flattened under heavy weights to make sheets.

You can see the writing on this ancient piece of papyrus.

Write your name in hieroglyphs

Hieroglyphs were either a whole word or a single letter.

The name of a pharaoh was written on an oval **cartouche**.

▶ Write your name in hieroglyphs and put it in a cartouche.

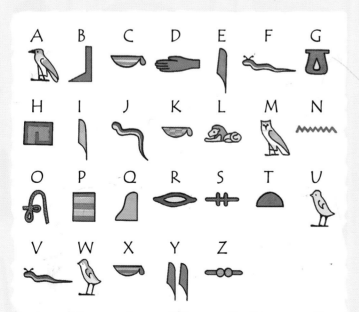

Gods and goddesses

The Ancient Egyptians worshipped many hundreds of gods and goddesses. They believed in life after death and tried to make sure they would get to the spirit world. Pharaohs went to a special place when they died called 'the land of the gods'.

The gods

Egyptians believed that the gods controlled human beings and all of nature.

The falcon-headed god Re is always shown with a golden disc.

Re was the sun god and creator of men.

Thoth, the moon god of wisdom, had a curved beak of a sacred ibis.

Horus, protector of Pharaohs, had a falcon's head.

Anubis was the jackal-headed god of death, rebirth and **mummification**.

Isis was the goddess of women and children.

Khnum was the ram-headed god of the Nile

Make a head of the cat goddess Bastet

Re's daughter, a cat called Bastet, was the goddess of the harvest.

▶ **1** Scrunch up some newspaper to make a fist-sized ball. Put it on top of a cardboard tube and fix it to the tube with masking tape.

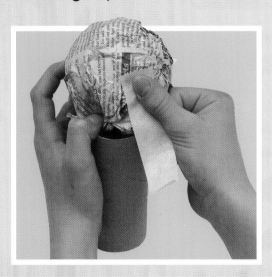

▶ **4** Cover the head with a layer of papier mâché. Leave to dry thoroughly.

▶ **5** Paint dark green all over and make the eyes yellow. Use gold paint to mark on earrings and a jewel on the forehead.

▶ **2** Mix a little PVA glue with water in a bowl. Tear up small pieces of newspaper and put them in the bowl to soak.

▶ **3** Shape two thick triangles from glue-soaked newspaper for ears and a strip for the nose. Fix with papier mâché strips.

The Pharaoh

The Pharaoh was the king of Egypt. The Egyptians believed that the Pharaoh was a god and that his wife was a goddess. A boy born to be the Pharaoh learnt to hunt, to fight and to lead his army in battle. The Pharaoh was also a high priest in the temple.

Famous Pharaohs

Ramses the Great built many great buildings and monuments. The ruins of these can still be seen today. Similarly, jewellery, clothes and weapons from the tomb of the Pharaoh Tutankhamun tell us a great deal about Ancient Egypt.

War

The Pharaoh went to war to protect his land against hostile armies or to take over another country. He rode in a horse-drawn chariot and carried a bow and arrow.

A carving of Ramses the Great.

A picture of Tutankhamun riding to war in a chariot.

A Pharaoh had coloured crowns for different occasions. He wore different-coloured crowns in different parts of Egypt, and another colour in times of war.

This painting on a coffin shows a Pharaoh's crown.

Make a Pharaoh's blue crown

▶ **1** Copy and cut out the shape of the crown on blue card. Make it about the width of your head.

▶ **2** Decorate it with gold spots, a coiled cobra and a golden sun disk.

▶ **3** Make a band of gold card to go around your head. Attach the blue crown and wear it.

Temple life

Egyptian temples were huge. They were built of stone because they were meant to last forever. Priests performed temple rituals, such as offering gifts to the gods. Only high priests and the Pharaoh went into the inner temple. Ordinary people were allowed into the temple courtyard for festivals.

Temple walls were painted and carved with stories of gods and Pharaohs.

Around the temple

The temple gate was called a pylon. Statues of the Pharaoh stood at the gate. Tall, thin **obelisks** carved with messages to the gods marked the point where the first rays of the sun fell. **Sphinxes** guarded the avenue in front of the temple.

A sphinx had a lion's body and the head of a man.

The hour watcher priest

The hour watcher priest was in charge of making sure the temple rituals were carried out on time. By day, he kept time by the sun. At night, he used a water clock. Water dripped slowly from a hole in the bottom of a special container. It took an hour for water to drop from one mark to the next.

A water clock from Ancient Egypt.

Make a water clock

▶ 1 Make a very small hole in the base of a large paper cup with a safety pin (ask an adult to help).

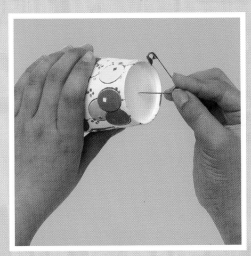

▶ 2 Tape some black paper around the cup. Decorate it with Egyptian figures and hieroglyphs.

▶ 3 Fill the cup with water and suspend it in a tall glass.

▶ 4 How long does it take to empty? Mark the level of the water every 5 minutes with a waterproof pen on the inside of the cup.

The pyramids

Egypt's great **pyramids** were tombs for some of the Pharaohs and their families. Each Pharaoh's body was laid in a chamber deep inside the pyramid where it was protected from the heat, and from robbers and animals. The burial chamber was filled with things the Pharaoh would need in the **afterlife**.

The pyramid shape

The shape of the pyramid was built to look like the mound that rose from water at the beginning of time, as told in Egyptian **myths**. The sun god Re stood on the mound's peak and called up all the other gods and goddesses.

The four sides of a pyramid faced north, south, east and west.

The great pyramid

The great pyramid at Giza is about 4,500 years old. It was the tomb of King Khufu. The workers building the pyramid had no pulleys, only levers and rollers to move two million blocks of stone. It took about 20 years to build one huge pyramid.

The insides of burial chambers were decorated with pictures and writing.

Make a pyramid

▶ 1 Copy the pattern of a four-sided pyramid onto yellow card and cut out. Include a flap on one edge.

▶ 2 Fold along the dotted lines and stick the flap to form a pyramid shape.

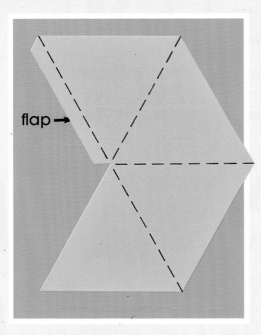

flap →

▶ 3 Paint details on the pyramid. You could add a burial chamber in a small box inside.

The afterlife

The Ancient Egyptians believed in life after death. They thought they needed their body in the afterlife so they took great care to **preserve** dead bodies. This was done by a process called mummification.

Mummification

Mummification was carried out by **embalmers**. The heart was left in the body. The brain was pulled out through the nose with a hook.

This wall painting shows the embalmers at work mummifying bodies.

Anubis, the jackal-headed god, was god of mummification.

The lungs, stomach, intestines and liver were removed, dried and put in **canopic jars**.

The body was dried, the face was made up and a wig was put on.

Then the body was rubbed with scented oil, covered in **resin** and wrapped in linen.

The canopic jars were protected by the four sons of the god Horus.

This jar has the head of Duamatef, the jackal-headed god.

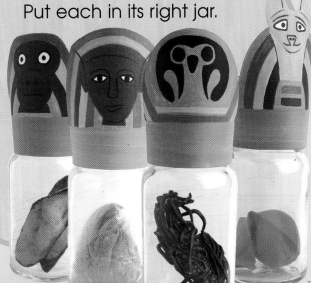

Make canopic jars with dried vital organs

▶ **1** Find four small glass jars. Copy the pictures of the four sons of Horus onto strips of paper to decorate your jars.

Hapi – baboon-headed god who protected the lungs.

Duamutef – jackal-headed god who protected the stomach.

▶ **2** To make the lungs, cut out shapes of lungs in orange peel and dry them out. For the stomach, blow up a small pink balloon then let out the air.

▶ **3** Make the intestines by painting dried noodles brown and dark red. The liver is a dried-out used tea bag or coffee filter wrapped in cling film. Put each in its right jar.

Qebehsenuef – falcon-headed god who protected the intestines.

Imsety – human-headed god who protected the liver.

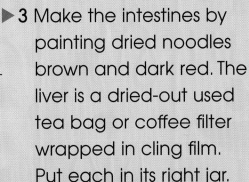

27

Glossary

Afterlife

Life after death. The Egyptians believed they lived on in another place after they died.

Amulet

Charms worn as a protection against evil spirits.

Anklet

Jewellery worn around the ankle.

Canopic jar

A jar used in Ancient Egypt to hold organs of the body.

Civilisation

An organised society, usually based around a city.

Embalmer

Someone who treats a dead body to stop it decaying.

Engineer

Someone who designs and builds buildings and machines.

Goods

Things bought and sold such as food, cloth and jewels.

Hieroglyph

A symbol or picture used for writing. The Ancient Egyptians wrote in hieroglyphs.

Irrigation canals

Ditches carrying water from a lake or river to fields where crops grow.

Kilt

A pleated, knee-length skirt.

Linen

Cloth woven from threads spun from the flax plant.

Loin cloth

A cloth tied round the hips and between the legs.

Mummification

A way of keeping a dead body from decaying by treating it with oils and wrapping it in cloth.

Myth

An old story about gods and heroes in ancient times.

Noble

Someone with wealth and power in a royal court or government.

Obelisk

A monument in the shape of a flat-sided pillar with a pointed top like a pyramid.

Pharaoh

Kings of Ancient Egypt were called Pharaohs.

Preserve

To keep from decaying or rotting.

Pyramid

A shape with a square base and triangular walls. Some Egyptian royalty were buried in giant pyramids.

Resin

A sticky tree sap that was used by embalmers in mummification.

Scribe

Someone who writes documents by hand. Ancient Egyptian scribes wrote in hieroglyphs.

Silt

Tiny pieces of mud or clay carried along by rivers. Silt helps to make soil rich for farming.

Sphinx

A creature with a lion's body and the head of a man, a ram or a bird.

Tomb

A grave or a cave or building that contains a grave.

Index